All About Wood

Contents

Jennifer Prescott

What Is Good About Wood?

Wood is one of the most useful **materials** on earth.

This boat is being built from wood. It will help the boat float and move quickly over the water

Wood is also strong and sturdy enough to last in the wind and waves.

Wood is easy to work with. It can be sawed, cut, bent, and carved into almost any shape.

Paper and cardboard are made from wood that has been ground into **pulp**. Puzzles and boxes can be made from cardboard.

Where Do We Get Wood?

Wood is a **natural resource** that comes from trees.

1 First, trees are cut down in the forest.

2 Next, logs are loaded onto trucks and driven to the sawmill.

3 At the sawmill, the bark is removed.

4 Then computers help workers cut the logs into flat boards.

5 Now the lumber is stacked up and ready to use!

Who Works with Wood?

Carpenters build houses, cabinets, chairs, and tables with wood. These workers use saws, hammers, and other tools to cut wood and make it smooth.

Other woodworkers use tools to carve wood into beautiful shapes.

People in factories work with wood too. These pieces of wood will be made into baseball bats!

What Woods Do We Use?

A lightweight wood called balsa is often used to make **models** and toys. Why do you think this wood is good to use?

Most pencils are made of incense-cedar wood. This wood is soft, so you can easily sharpen the pencils.

Baseball bats are made from wood that will not crack or splinter, such as white ash.

People everywhere use wood to make all kinds of interesting and colorful things.

Masks and wooden eggs in South Africa

Korean man playing a *koto*, a wooden instrument

Dolls in Ukraine

Tlingit totem poles in Alaska, U.S.A.

How Can We Have Wood for the Future?

We can reuse wood. One way is to shred wood to make **mulch**. Mulch helps soil stay moist and stops weeds from growing.

Mulch

Paper comes from wood. We can **recycle** the paper we use so that none is wasted.

Wood is valuable—and **renewable**.

If we plant new trees to replace the ones we cut down, and take care of them as they grow we will always have wood to use.